AF440862

Generis
PUBLISHING

Biblical Etymology of Prophet and Priest

James Xianxing Du

Copyright © 2020 James Xianxing Du

Copyright © 2020 Generis Publishing

All rights reserved. This book or any portion thereof may not be reproduced or used in any manner whatsoever without the written permission of the publisher except for the use of brief quotations in a book review.

CIP a Camerei Naţionale a Cărţii

Du, James Xianxing. Biblical Etymology of Prophet and Priest / James Xianxing Du. – Chişinău : Generis Publishing, 2020 (Print on demand). – 64 p. Referinţe bibliogr.: p. 63-64 (23 tit.).
ISBN 978-9975-154-50-5.
27-29
D 86

Cover image: www.pixabay.com

Generis Publishing

Online orders: www.generis-publishing.com
Orders by email: info@generis-publishing.com

Table of Contents

Abstract

Regarding the origin of language, Genesis claims that ancient languages were divinely diversified. This testimony presents systematic evidence for biblical etymology related to prophet and priest. Priesthood was pivotal in ancient culture, and religious worship is central to civilization. This testimony presents systematic and surprising evidence for relationship of prophet and priest to biblical etymology, indicating that the old testament culture and method of worship are extensively reflected by etymology of words.

In multilingual match in biblical etymology to prophets and priests, junior is to join, sandal is sacred land, frog is to forbid going, flea and fly are to flee, mosquito has man in motion, 龟 turtle has altar 田 , bat has tabernacle, tangerine is to ignite, frame is lamb on fire to march away from Pharaoh, miracle is marine ram, wonder is no water, anecdote has dance, absence is sea dance, follow has flow, to decide is to dice and cede, to indicate is to cide and dice dedicated cattle, politic and police are to split offering and burn lipid, praise has separated pair, pray has ray and pair, priest is related to spirit, president is priest of residents, bureaucrat is related to tabernacle, 募 recruit is for curtain 幕, epidemic is epi dēmos, plague is for people to leave and go to another place, pandemic is to cide bird, infection is to confine, inflammation is in flame, fever is fire to offer, disease is to segregate aside, sick is to cut as related to sickle and scissor, hospital is distal site, pharmacy is far from camp, drug is to go, 醫 medicine is to cide 殳 and not at domain, quarantine is quadra plus ten, therapy is to heat and tear apart, to treat is to tear, 療 heal is to heat 燎 and leave, anger is no region, quarrel has liquid and quail, value is veal, price is spice, business is to combust incense, profit is pro fission, revenue is to sever and revere, to divide is dividend, to employ has temple, 聖 sacred and consecration have ear 耳, 職 career has ear 耳, 聘 hire in shrine has ear 耳, swear has ear and wear, and work is worship. The multilingual mutual match in biblical etymology definitively proves divine creation as the origin of language, and validates scriptures of Pentateuch and gospel. The etymological testimony proves THE CREATOR.

Keywords: priest, prophet, etymology, bible, anthropology, multilingual biblical match, creation, origin of language

I. Introduction

Last year, bible was proven to be the source of etymology in main human languages, a crucial discovery in the linguistic field [1-4]. From seven divine days to the great flood, multilingual analyses presented a series of evidence that languages have biblical etymology, and bible is the decoding book for semantic origin of words [2-7].

Genesis 11 claims that GOD "confused the language of the whole world" around Babel tower [1]. Accordingly, to confuse has secon of second, tower is two er, and tone is not (as) one (people). However, people want to find additional linguistic evidence for such confusion. After languages suddenly burst out around the time of Babel tower, people also want to know the real etymology of words. This testimony provides linguistic evidence that numerous words have obvious biblical etymology related to biblical prophets and priests.

II. Method

The basic method of this linguistic analysis is to consider that every native word in an ancient language is a riddle, in other words, logogriph. Subunits of every word are analyzed to see how they combine to form a meaningful word to match biblical events, decrees, worshipers and conversations in graphic and semantic organization. For every word with revealed biblical match, its translation in additional language is aligned with it, in order to decode the etymology of the translated word, if bilingual match exists for such a word. This mutual bilingual alignment is focused on words in English and their translations in the language of China, but many words derived from Latin, Greek, German, French and additional languages are also involved. In addition, linkage analysis is also performed by interconnecting different words together to match identical biblical origin, strengthening the conclusion that etymology of native words is from bible, and languages were initially divinely created.

III. Results

3.1 Prophet

3.1.1 Etymology of prophet

Prophet is people with radiant light. Prophet has phote of photo, an affix of light in photon, photosynthesis, photocopy, photoelectric and photograph, because in Exodus 3:1-34:35 GOD called to Moses from within the burning bush on Horeb mountain, and his "face was radiant, and they were afraid"—phobic [10]. Prophesy/prophecy has phos as firelight in phosphate, phosphorus and phosphorescence, and is related to phoenix, the mythical bird resurrecting from fire.

Prophet (先知)'s ancient version in the language of China, 耑 知 (prophet), has 止 (legs) to be banned to step forward 屮 in the wild 耑. 一 sometimes indicates prohibition, 屮 is footstep, and 矢 矢 (arrow) represents the wild [4]. Moses was divinely informed, "Do not come any closer". "Take off your sandals, for the place where you are standing is holy ground". 口

mouth is also included, as prophet talks, although it can represent altar too. 先 羌 (prior) is in wash 洗 濺, because priests must wash themselves, as represented by legs 足 with water 水 prior to entering Tent of Meeting. Otherwise, it is 一 forbidden to step into, as represented by 止 (footstep). In Exodus 30:18-40:32, "Aaron and his sons are to wash their hands and feet with water from it. Whenever they enter the Tent of Meeting, they shall wash with water so that they will not die. Also, when they approach the altar to minister by presenting an offering made to THE LORD by fire, they shall wash their hands and feet so that they will not die. This is to be a lasting ordinance for Aaron and his descendants for the generations to come." "He placed the basin between the Tent of Meeting and the altar and put water in it for washing, and Moses and Aaron and his sons used it to wash their hands and feet. They washed whenever they entered the Tent of Meeting or approached the altar, as THE LORD commanded Moses."

Since first fruit of harvest is offered in Deuteronomy 26:1-10, Numbers 15:18-18:28 and Leviticus 2:14-16 [11, 12, 13], harvest is to serve at altar by human. Starve is arvest of harvest. In etymology, to starve is related to harvest, as seven years of harvest preceded seven years of starvation. In Genesis 41:17-29, Joseph prophesied that "Seven years of great abundance are coming throughout the land of Egypt, but seven years of famine will follow them" [1]. Prophesy has oseph of Joseph coincidentally.

旋 㲋 (swirl/helix) has two prophets, 㲋 Elisha and 乚 Elijah who rose up 人. In 2 Kings 2:1-12, "LORD was about to take Elijah up to heaven in a whirlwind". "Elijah went up to heaven in a whirlwind. Elisha saw this and cried out" [14]. Swirl is to rise in wind. Elijah and Elisha have heli of helix. 漩 whirlpool is derived from whirl. The genetic code of life, DNA, is double stranded helix. Elijah received his eternal life in helical way.

In Genesis 2:2, "on the seventh day HE rested from all HIS WORK". In Matthew 11:13, "For all the prophets and the Law prophesied until John". Jesus Christ claims that GOD will not come back until the end of this world [1, 15-18]. Accordingly, GOD does not physically arrive to directly call a prophet any more until the end of this heaven and earth. Prophet is a term of polysemy when Paul mentioned Son's prophets, calling through Holy Spirit, or spiritual predictors in broader sense.

Apostle Paul links to photo, light, although he was only the prophet of Son of GOD as in Matthew 11:13 "For all the prophets and the law prophesied until John". In Acts 9:1-18 [19], "As he neared Damascus on his journey, suddenly a light from heaven flashed around him. He fell to the ground and heard a Voice say to him, "Saul, Saul, why do you persecute Me?""

3.1.2 Veil of Moses

"When Moses finished speaking to them, he put a veil over his face. But whenever he entered THE LORD'S PRESENCE to speak with him, he removed the veil until he came out." "Then Moses would put the veil back over his face until he went in to speak with THE LORD". Thus, 巾 veil (巾 as its seal version) is to be removed (丨) in Tent of Meeting (冂). Veil is related to leave, as Moses put on veil when leaving Tent of Meeting. 帕 veil has light from altar 凸, and 幕 curtain and screen have 莫 no (ni/ne) scarf 巾, because curtains form the entrance to 冂 Tent of Meeting, while Moses removed veil when entering it. Because Moses' "face was radiant, and they were afraid", cloth has chlo to shine after exiting shrine, and scarf is related to scare. 怖, phobia and dreadful, also has to dress veil 巾/布, as the people were afraid. Therefore, linguistic anthropology presents etymological evidence for biblical events in archaeology.

As a bilingual match, 募 (募 as its ancient version), to recruit, has curti of curtain 幕, tricolor yarn ♥, and designated place ⊟, as in Exodus 35:4-29 Moses recruited women and their gifts [10]. "Everyone who had blue, purple or scarlet yarn or fine linen, or goat hair, ram skins dyed red or hides of sea cows brought them." "Every skilled woman spun with her hands and brought what she had spun—blue, purple or scarlet yarn or fine linen."

帥 chief (Moses) has veil 巾, when going from one place to another as represented by the relocation affix ⺆ (from Tent to altar, for instance). 篩 sift has the chief (帥) to perform fission of offering indicated by symmetric ⺮. In other words, it is not a coincidence that bilingually sift has fission. Correspondingly, sift's noun, sieve, is to sever and serve offering, related to veil and chief too. The semantic relationship among sift, fission, sieve and sever is due to biblical burnt altar's bronze network between offering and fire. In Exodus 27:5 and 38:4, "They made a grating for the altar, a bronze network, to be under its ledge, halfway up the altar." This grating network can be considered as a filter. Thus, filter has fire at altar in etymology. In addition, filter is fission near eltr (altar).

The copper grating of biblical burnt altar ⌗ exists abundantly in Maya language. There is no doubt that Maya language must have bible as its source of etymology, and was divinely created [2]. Unfortunately, in the past some Mayan graphs and affixes of copper grating were confused with turtle shell and shield, although turtle does involve burnt altar: turtle has eltur of altar, and is even read as true eltur. A similar word is culture 尚/俗, which has ultur as altar 囗. The translation of turtle, 龟, also has altar's network 田 [2]. Turtle shell was apparently created to remind mankind the solid network of burnt altar, and turtle lives for hundreds of years of peaceful long life. In many cultures, turtle either is very spiritual or symbolizes fortune, as creatures were created in symbolic implication and their words frequently match biblical etymology [2-7].

Shield also involves altar, although in this case it is incense altar involved. The altar of incense was behind the shielding curtain of Tent of Meeting, close to the curtain that shielded ark in Most Holy Place. In Leviticus 16:11-14, "He is to take a censer full of burning coals from the altar before THE LORD and two handfuls of finely ground fragrant incense and take them behind the curtain. He is to put the incense on the fire before THE LORD, and the smoke of the incense will conceal the atonement cover above the testimony". Among the translations of shield, 盾 shield contains 目 that resembles an altar (囗) with offering (二). As a biblical weapon, shield's alternative etymology is elbow dish, a dish ○ with two handles 二 held by elbow.

The other translation of sieve, sift and filter, 濾, also has burnt altar with bronze grating 田. It also has the affix of piety 虍, two worshipers 㕚 at two sides of Tent of Meeting 厂 western to burnt altar 田 [4]. To the surprise, this word's major structure 慮 means to conceive and consider. Biblical etymology answers such puzzles: 慮 consideration has second and dice to section, because offerings were cut to two by Abraham in Genesis 15:10. "Abram brought all these to him, cut them in two and arranged the halves opposite each other" [1]. A similar word is decision. 判 to decide is to dice and cede in halves 半, and decision has second dice.

As indisputable evidence for divine creation as the origin of languages, biblical etymology can answer all puzzles in relationship of words. For instance, why in writing shift links to fission, and in translation move 移 has more 多? The answer is Leviticus. 移 shift has fission of meat as indicated by 多, although transfer of grain offering (禾 means crop such as wheat) is additional etymology. 移, to move things from one place to another, has more 多 多 to match fission and section, because the cut offering needs to be removed from the place of dissection and moved to altar to be heated. Wheat and flour are burnt at altar as offering, so that wheat has heat, flour is related to fire, and grain offering is related to grating.

17

3.1.3 Staff of Moses

In the first sign and miracle to Pharaoh, Moses and Aaron turned staff to snake. In Exodus 4:2-7:12, LORD said to Moses, ""What do you have in your hand?" "A wooden staff," he said. THE LORD said, "Throw it on the ground." So Moses threw it on the ground. It turned into a snake. He ran away from it. Then THE LORD said to Moses, "Reach your hand out. Take the snake by the tail." So he reached out and grabbed hold of the snake. It turned back into a staff in his hand." "Pharaoh will say to you, 'Do a miracle.' When he does, speak to Aaron. Tell him, 'Take your wooden staff and throw it down in front of Pharaoh.' It will turn into a snake." "Each one threw his staff down. Each staff turned into a snake. But Aaron's staff swallowed theirs up." Thus, snake transnotes scepter and in turn, worshiper with such staff, in a subset of words.

In multilingual biblical match, both 濾 filter and affiliation 属 have Tent of Meeting, also termed tabernacle, in side view 厂. 属 affiliation (屬 as its ancient version) is staff under Tent 尸 (side view of Tent of Meeting). In Exodus 2:11-33:11, Moses stood at the entrance to the camp and said,

"Whoever is for THE LORD, come to me." The staff can be directly seen in the ancient versions 㼝 㫃, as 𝔶 and 𝔯 are snake 蛇, and ⊓ and ⊢ are scepter. Their coexistence in 属 is from mutual transformation between scepter and serpent in Exodus 4:2-5. "Moses reached out and took hold of the snake and it turned back into a staff in his hand" [10]. The other translation of 属, belong to, is to go on belly to transnote Moses' staff, as snake crawls on belly. However, blood on earlobe is also an etymology of belong, as Moses put blood on earlobes of consecrated priests. 瞩, to fix eyes to behold, is a related word, when the consecration ceremony was watched over. "As Moses went into the tent, the pillar of cloud would come down and stay at the entrance, while THE LORD spoke with Moses. Whenever the people saw the pillar of cloud standing at the entrance to the tent, they all stood and worshiped" to 瞩 fix eyes on.

Scepter is serpect of serpent. As 丁 𝔯 are scepter according to linguists' traditional interpretation [20], adding altar 凵 to scepter gives rise to can 可 可 可 , which means that something can be approved or accepted. In alternative etymology, 可 (can) is to ban (as indicated by 一) Red sea or Jordan river ⟨, so that altar 凵 could be carried across. In this regards, the word "can" could be considered as no (an 一) water wave (⌣ or ⟨ represented by letter c), although can's primary etymology is to burn burnt offering [2-4]. This is why can is related to candle, cannon and canon. Due to the biblical division of offering before burning the cut sections at altar, it brings no surprise that the past and past perfect tenses of the modal verb can, could, has duol of double. In apparent bilingual mutual match, 能, can and could, has grapheme 匕 in double and duality 㠯. In other words, in etymology 能 can is related to contrast and comparison 比 比比.

Moses' elder brother 哥 (哥 as its ancient version) Aaron also had an approved scepter 丆 as almond staff near altar 凵, since in Numbers 17:5 "The staff belonging to the man I choose will sprout" [12]. In the language of China, there are specific words to distinguish between elder and younger siblings. The duplicated structure in elder brother 哥 fully correlates with Aaron as the elder brother of Moses to hold the additional staff, indicating the accuracy in created words to reflect biblical authenticity. 寄 is to live at another place, as Hebrews were aliens in Egypt and Moses lived in Midian as an alien. 吁 吁 sigh has water from sky and earth for man to vanquish in water. 汰 汰 vanquish has man 大 at Red sea or great flood 巛. Sigh is for water to go over human, and vanquish is aqui vanish.

包 (勹 as its ancient version), to wrap around, has staff of snake 巳 巳 巳 and bowing person 勹 [20], and involves either Moses who wrapped around his head with veil to cover radiant face, or Aaron who wrapped ark with curtain. In Numbers 4:5, "when the camp is to move, Aaron and his sons are to go in and take down the shielding curtain and cover the ark of the Testimony with it." In Numbers 17:8, "Aaron's staff, which represented the house of Levi, had not only sprouted but had budded, blossomed and produced almonds". Thus, 苞 bud has worshiper 勹 with the transnoted scepter to match biblical event, not only for petals to wrap around 包. Even if 巳 is 己, it can still have snake ㄹ and staff ㅣ.

跑 to run also demonstrates such deeply embedded biblical etymology. In the past millenniums, everyone was puzzled by why running 跑 has to 包 wrap foot 足. Now it is not a puzzle any more, as its etymology is for 勹 Moses to run (跑) away from his staff when it turned to snake 巳. This turn to run is recorded in Exodus 4 in the calling of Moses [10]. Moses also took his entire clan to run away from Egypt, so that 包 envelope is related to elope 跑. Chief rabbi was chef to barbecue cut offering in front of Tent of Meeting 厂 (side view), as recorded in Exodus and Leviticus of old testament. In other words, 庖 chef originally might not wrap roll or burrito but involved Moses with scepter. There is an ancient idiom 庖丁解牛, chef to cut apart ox. In the past three millenniums, it was all considered as butchering an ox for cuisine. Now in biblical origin it ought to be considered as dissection of an ox for worship!

Moses 勹 and his staff of snake ꝋ also transnote cloak 袍, derived from the second sign to Moses in Exodus 4:6-7. "LORD said, "Put your hand inside your cloak." So Moses put his hand into his cloak, and when he took it out, it was leprous, like snow. "Now put it back into your cloak," HE said. So Moses put his hand back into his cloak, and when he took it out, it was restored, like the rest of his flesh". In Exodus 7:14-24, "take in your hand the staff that was changed into a snake. Then say to him, "THE LORD, THE GOD of the Hebrews, has sent me to say to you: Let my people go"". "Tell Aaron, 'Take your staff and stretch out your hand over the waters' 'and they will turn to blood'." Relevant to ꝋ worshiper's staff ꝋ, 礮 泡 immerse is in serum 淵 for fingers 勹 to dig 刨 魝, as then "all the Egyptians dug along the Nile to get drinking water".

3.1.4 Burning bush

榮 glory has fire 火, 宀 mountain and the affix of plant 木 related to LORD 禾 禼. 棘 朿朿 bush, shrub or brush is human (h) next to combustion (bus of combustion and moxibustion 灸 is an affix of fire). These are because in

Exodus 3:1-6 "the angel of THE LORD appeared to him in flames of fire from within a bush" on Horeb mountain. "GOD called to him from within the bush, "Moses! Moses!"". "Take off your sandals, for the place where you are standing is holy ground." Sandal is removed in sanctuary, and in definitive etymology sandal is sacred land and saint land. 蠑螈 salamander, salamandre in French, and salamandra in Latin and Greek have sandal realm. Its traditional etymology of creature that lives with fire matches the call to Moses, as "though the bush was on fire it did not burn up" [10]. It also has land of plain 原, as GOD promised Moses to "bring them up out of that land into a good and spacious land".

鯢 giant salamander or baby fish has fish 鱼, basket 臼 and son 兒. It has big head symbolizing infant, four legs, weight of a child, and distinct voice resembling infant's cry. Baby Moses floated on Nile river, and salamander lives in clean water to cry like a baby. 娃 children of GOD walked on both land and Red Sea, and frog 蛙 and salamander 娃娃鱼 live both on land and in water. These words all share the affix 圭, from one ground to another ground 土 (from Egypt to Canaan), although 圭's ancient version is interpreted as 土 ground (一) banning entry 屮. In other words, 娃 child has forbidden land as the alternative etymology, when the first recorded biblical child Cain was born outside the forbidden Eden garden and driven away from the land. When Moses reached 120 years of full age, he was forbidden to enter the promised land Canaan. That generation, except Joshua and Caleb, failed to enter until the next generation, as in Numbers 14:21-30 and Deuteronomy 1:32-40 "not one of the men who saw MY GLORY and the miraculous signs I performed in Egypt and in the desert but who disobeyed ME and tested ME ten times—not one of them will ever see the land I promised on oath". Accordingly, 恚 anger has the ban to enter a land 圭, anger is an region, and anger is an (not) ge (go) er. The chronological order of these words and the relevant affix match time line of biblical events.

Additional words also nicely interlink through this land prohibition and relocation affix 圭. 桂 cinnamon has no man in. 挂 to suspend or hang can involve the forbidden fruit on the tree of Eden. 洼, depression with water, is where should not be walked. 闺 boudoir is lady's bedroom to ban entry of outsiders. 崖 cliff is the margin that cannot be walked over. To prevent walking over water's edge 涯 to drown, edge is eg de, go away from. 蛙 viper has man banned to enter but relocated to another ground (out of Eden garden or in Exodus). 封 𡨄 to block is not to 一 locate 屮 to a ground 土 by divine hand 彐, as Eden garden was closed and the couple had to relocate to second location. Closure is to relocate. In apparent etymology for the calling of Moses when sandals were written in bible in limited cases, the sacred ground is also in good 佳 and sandal 鞋, as Moses took off sandals at holy ground of Horeb and was not allowed to 跬 step closer forward when divinely called.

Ancient names typically have biblical etymology [2-7]. For instance, surname Du 杜 can represent 木 bush at holy ground 土. Ancient version 米凸 has plant 米 at a stony region △ preventing (一) Moses from moving forward ǀ at the holy ground △. 防 阝 prevention has 夕 worshiper Moses with the affix of region from one place (▱) to another (▱) 阝. To prevent is to step (vent) front (pre), derived from prae venire of Latin as a multilingual match to bible. In Exodus 3:2-4:9 Moses thought, "I will go over and see this strange sight—why the bush does not burn up." When THE LORD saw that he had gone over to look, GOD called to him from within the bush, "Moses! Moses!" "Do not come any closer," GOD said. "Take off your sandals, for the place where you are standing is holy ground." The flowers of mountain shrub Sims Azalea 杜鹃 look like fire with mountain red, as "Moses saw that though the bush was on fire it did not burn up". As the most distinctive feature, some cuckoo 杜鹃 lays egg of her child on other bird's nest to be raised up by the adopting bird, as Moses' mother left him to be adopted by Pharaoh's daughter. Around summer cuckoo cries days and nights, as Moses cried and Pharaoh gave this order:

"Every boy that is born you must throw into the Nile". A lot of ancient poems described cuckoo's mournful cry, for instance, 杜鹃啼血, cuckoo cries blood. The greatest prophet Moses' cry 啼 was related to GOD 帝 [13]. This phenomenon of the same compound word to represent both a plant and a bird, which were created to symbolize biblical Moses, can only be interpreted by divine creation of words with statistical probability beyond nature.

Prevention is also in two additionally related compound words, one of which is an idiom. 防微杜渐 , caution beforehand before onset of significant error or misfortune, can be read literally as to prevent (防) tiny (微) Moses' killing (斩) at water (氵 氵) ("Birth of Moses" in the next section). 杜绝, to put an end to, is to put an end to the slavery of Moses' people, before Pharaoh put an end to them by murdering Hebrew boys at Nile river. In Exodus 1:16, "When you help the Hebrew women in childbirth and observe them on the delivery stool, if it is a boy, kill him; but if it is a girl, let her live." 绝 has several meanings including extremely or to terminate, and can be read literally as colored (色) textile (纟糸帛), since Moses put a veil on his radiant face and must have worn colored garment as a high priest, and curtains of tabernacle installed by Moses and priestly textiles such as ephod must have twisted tricolor yarn or cloth of color

[10-12].

Another related word is 捐 donation, which has an apparent altar 口 and sacrificed flesh 肙, as Moses collected donation and donated offers in worship, described extensively in old testament. "All the Israelite men and women who were willing brought to THE LORD freewill offerings". "When the altar was anointed, the leaders brought their offerings for its dedication and presented them before the altar" with two pages of donations in Exodus 35:1-36:7 and Numbers 7:3-88 [10, 12]. The ancient 杜 杜 can also be considered as plant 木 near a primary altar on ground 土. This altar has been substituted with copper grating of burnt altar 十 or cross. Addition of altar 口 is orange and tangerine 桔, as tangerine (egnate+rin) has ignite, and orange has egna of ignition in etymology, because sections of orange and tangerine resemble flame ⑩. In one etymology, sign (signe in French and signum in Latin) is igniting fire, such as burning stars created as signs in Genesis [1]. 桔 orange, including tangerine, was obviously created to be reminiscent of burnt offering of biblical worship, and has blessing and luck 吉. As orange and sign are derived from multiple languages, these indicate identical design in initial emergence of languages.

3.1.5 Birth of Moses

In Exodus 2:1-10 [10], when a Levite woman could not further hide his son under Pharaoh's decree, "she got a papyrus basket for him and coated it with tar and pitch. Then she placed the child in it and put it along the reeds along the bank of the Nile." Pharaoh's daughter saw the basket and rescued the baby. "He was crying, and she felt sorry". She named him Moses, saying, "I drew him out of water." 棄 (灥 彙 as ancient versions), to abandon, has child 孒 ♦ Moses, ∵ water of Nile river, ⊌ 甾 basket, and ʸ ˣ ᵖ˞ two hands of the maid of Pharaoh's daughter. As one etymology, 兒 son also has this basket 臼 near a human being represented by two legs. Not listening to her earthly king, Pharaoh's daughter showed the greatest bravery and conscience, blessing Egypt through her.

棄 abandon can also be considered to contain winnow 𠦝 or certain utensil that holds parts of ox 廾. It is related to finish 畢 畢, as at the end of ceremony priest took dissected bull "outside the camp to a place ceremonially clean, where the ashes are thrown, and burnt it in a wood fire" [11]. This place is concentrated with leftover, so that 篝火 campfire has 莽, which has ox next to ox (屮 or 㞢). 畚 scoop is for ashes of burnt altar 田. 溝 ditch has flock next to flock 㞢 to 覯/遘 meet and mate 媾, as in Genesis 30:31-42 Jacob "placed the peeled branches in all the watering troughs".

"When the flocks were in heat and came to drink, they mated in front of the branches" [1]. 購 is to buy flock after flock. Jacob bought such wage by his work day and night to Laban. "Let me go through all your flocks today and remove from them every speckled or spotted sheep, every dark-colored lamb and every spotted or speckled goat. They will be my wages."

3.1.6 Miracles to Pharaoh

3.1.6.1 Frogs

In Exodus 8:1-14, "Let MY people go, so that they may worship ME." "The Nile will teem with frogs. They will come up into your palace and your bedroom and onto your bed, into the houses of your officials and on your people, and into your ovens and kneading troughs". 蛙 frog is for going or to forbid going 㳒 to a land 土, related to going from the land of Egypt to land of Canaan.

3.1.6.2 Gnats

In Exodus 8:16-18, "Tell Aaron, 'Stretch out your staff and strike the dust of

the ground,' and throughout the land of Egypt the dust will become gnats."
蚤 flea is to flee and has ⟍ hand and dust ⸪, and gnats include louse
虱 that has ⊐ hand, | staff and ଛଛ gnats. 蠓 gnat has sacrificed bull
head 艹 and two persons 从 Moses and Aaron, and the land was 滿 full of
them. 蚊 mosquito has man in motion 㐱, gnat is for a nation to go, louse
has to relocate, and flea has to flee at Passover.

3.1.6.3 Flies

In Exodus 8:20-29, "Dense swarms of flies poured into Pharaoh's palace
and into the houses of his officials". Then Pharaoh summoned Moses and
Aaron and said, "Go, sacrifice to your GOD here in the land." But Moses
replied that we "must take a three-day journey into the desert to offer
sacrifices to THE LORD our GOD". In etymology, fly is to flee, derived
from this miracle before Hebrews fled away from oppression. 蠅 fly is also
consistent with the third miracle of frog 黽, including 口 altar and either
movement through door or two hands to present offering, because in
etymology door 門 (門) has tricolor cord 绳 (represented by ∈ ∋) of Tent
of Meeting's curtain. Frogs passed through all doors. Flies too. Fruit fly is
drosophila, and droso is doors in regrouped letters. Phila is plant to love the
tree of life, although lovers Eve and Adam chose tree of wisdom. Spiritual

wisdom is to fully love GOD and to love each other, but earthly wisdom often leads to invention of killing weapons. This is one of the rationales why tree of wisdom was forbidden.

3.1.6.4 Plague on livestock

In Exodus 9:3-7, "LORD will bring a terrible plague on your livestock in the field". This epidemic 疫 killed (cide 殳) cattle 爿. The etymology of epidemic and pandemic is to cide bird, as a bird is killed in offering above water container [11]. Similar to epiderm as the outside of dermal layer, in additional etymology epidemic is epi dēmos, outside the domestic, because biblical patients of skin infection must leave camp and were isolated outside of camp [11]. Derived from this biblical Leviticus regulation, in etymology plague is for a person to leave, plague is to go (to another) place, infection is to confine, pestilence is to separate, and hospital is distal site. The Latinized Greek pharmaco- of pharmaceutical, pharmacy and pharmacology is far from camp. Drug is to go (gu) rural (ru/ur) to be banned in urban area, and quarantine has quadra- (four) and tein (ten/teen) to be fourteen days, as sometimes seven plus seven days of isolation are required to clean leprosy patients [11], although forty days were in practice centuries ago.

Additional words related to therapy and medicine are also from Leviticus. Medicine is to cide (kill bird). In addition, medicine is not (ne) at domain (camp). The translation of medicine, 醫, contains water container (酉 酉) to hold blood of the bird to be killed (cided 殳), and a distant rural area (區's affix 匸) represented by arrow (矢 矢 矢), perfectly consistent with Leviticus regulation to prove divine origin of words. The arrow has arro of rural and often represents countryside due to archer Esau's hunting at countryside [1-4]. 疾 (疒 疾) disease has arrow 矢 to represent outside isolation. 病 disease is to go from a converged place (一) to be diverged (as indicated by the symbol 人) to the outside, as represented by the affix of region 冂. 症 disease has inhibited (as represented by the horizontal line 一) footstep (止, 止), because leprosy patients are forbidden to enter camp [11]. 患, to be sick, is from one place (口) to another place (口), with the vertical line to indicate direction, as skin infectious patients are isolated outside of camp.

In dual etymologies that both match bible, therapy is both to heat (burnt offering) and to tear apart garment, and to treat is to tear, as old testament requires leprosy patients to offer burnt offering and tear garments [2-7, 11]. By the same token, 療 heal is both to heat 燎 and to leave camp. 恙 (ill and ail) has offered lamb 羊, clinic is to incinerate offering, inflammation is in flame, fever is fire to offer, disease is to segregate aside, disorder is not only dis order but also to be ordered to a distant side, and sick is to scki (schi is divide, a root also in sickle, scissor and schizophrenia), because burnt offering must be cut before burning. 瘟 epidemic has temperature 温 because of burnt offering at altar 日 , rather than fever as previously considered. 疒 疒, the common affix of diseases, has one side of offered flock or herd 爿, which was interpreted in the past as bed to confuse the language. These medical terms indisputably prove old testament and divine creation as the origin of languages.

3.1.6.5 Boils and hails

In Exodus 9:9-11 "festering boils broke out on men and animals." Moses' eighth miracle was hail. In Exodus 9:18-25 "Stretch out your hand toward the sky so that hail will fall all over Egypt—on men and animals and on everything". "When Moses stretched out his staff toward the sky, THE LORD sent thunder and hail". "LORD rained hail on the land". "Throughout Egypt hail struck everything in the fields—both men and animals", so that hail has h as human to leave and ail as livestock. 恙 ail has lamb 羊 [3]. As Moses stretched out his staff, 雹 (hail) and 疱 (boil) have worshiper 勹 with staff of snake 已 己 巳 to flee (跑) away from slavery in delivery.

3.1.6.6 Locusts in wind

In Exodus 10:1-20, 惶 frighting miracle of locust in wind was sent to Egyptian emperor, so that 蝗 locust has emperor 皇, and 風 wind has insect 虫 ઈ that also represents Moses' staff of snake. 虫 (ઈ as its ancient version) initially referred to snake as known by linguists [20], but also represents creatures such as worms, insects and even tiger (大虫). ઈ 虫 can also represent worshiper. In a set of words, it transnotes a worshiper with divinely provided authority, for instance, Moses with his staff of snake.

瘋 mad has a structure similar to wind 風. Wind is no water and water dwindles, as in Genesis 8:1-7 GOD "sent a wind over the earth, and the waters receded" [1]. This biblical verse is also the etymology of dwindle. In John 3:8, "The wind blows wherever it pleases...So it is with everyone born of The Spirit" [18]. In addition, Jesus Christ's direct disciples (not disciples in later generations) received powerful Holy Spirit sounding like wind in Pentecost. However, they were considered to be drunken, and a couple of apostles were thought to be insane in Acts, so that mad has wind.

楓 maple also has related semantic structure. Its leaves resemble mountain 山, as "on the seventeenth day of the seventh month the ark came to rest on the mountains of Ararat" [1]. Maple has palm to symbolize Noah's hand in wind. Its leaves turn red in autumn, the season when ark anchored on the mountain.

Linguists thought that honey/nectar 蜜 has insect 虫, as bee is an insect. However, 虫 also represents Moses' staff of snake, and to the surprise this word represents the divine promise of the journey and residency (represented by tent 宀 冂) onto a land flowing with honey. The land shown to Moses was flowing with milk and honey [10]. 宓 settlement is represented by Tent of Meeting, and honey is related to journey. 蜜 nectar has certan of certain 必, as GOD certainly achieved this promise [10, 21]. For thousands of years linguists thought that honeybee must be in its nest to make honey, but this testimony provides biblical etymology.

3.1.6.7 Darkness

In exodus 10:21-26, "Moses stretched out his hand toward the sky, and total darkness covered all Egypt for three days. No one could see anyone else or move about for three days. Yet all the Israelites had light in the places where they lived." 燈 lamp has flame 火, oil on container 豆, and two steps 癶 to represent Passover and migration in Exodus. Lamps preceded lambs of Passover [10].

When Pharaoh required to "only leave your flocks and herds behind", Moses replied that "You must allow us to have sacrifices and burnt offerings to present to THE LORD our GOD. Our livestock too must go with us; not a hoof is to be left behind. We have to use some of them in worship". Accordingly, 旰 ᵉ dark is to char herd 午, 昧 dark has 午 ox (represented by head with horns) on firewood 木, and 暗 dark has 午 ox on altar 日.

3.1.6.8 Passover

In Exodus 12:2-23, Hebrews "slaughter the Passover lamb. Take a bunch of hyssop, dip it into the blood in the basin and put some of the blood on the top and on both sides of the doorframe." LORD "will pass over that doorway". In Deuteronomy 6:4-11:20, "Love THE LORD your GOD with all your heart and with all your soul and with all your strength." "Write them on the doorframes". In full consistence with Passover, frame is lamb meat on fire, frame is to march away from Pharaoh, and frame 框 is to divinely pass (as represented by the footstep-derived affix 止) over door 门, by KING 王 to king. 匡 is to rectify and save. Israelites offer firstfruit basket 筐, memorizing the salvation in Deuteronomy 26:1-10 [13]. The passover lamb 羔 has 羊 lamb and 灬, the affix of fire, as it was "roasted over the fire, along with bitter herbs, and bread made without yeast. Do not eat the meat raw or cooked in water, but roast it over the fire".

3.1.7 Etymology of miracle and wonder

In etymology, miracle is related to marine, ram and Miriam, because of crossing Red sea by Israelites and their flocks and herds. The etymology of wonder is no water. 奇 奇 wonder has 大 man near altar 口 to hold staff 丁 to ban (一) water 氵, as Moses performed the miracle to divide sea and expose dry ground. 騎 ride or drive has 大 man to ride donkey 馬 and stop (一) water 氵, and is related to dried ground, as in Exodus 4:20 "Moses took his wife and sons, put them on a donkey and started back to Egypt. And he took the staff of GOD in his hand" [10]. Wane is ne wa, no water, as "By the first day of the first month of Noah's six hundred and first year, the water had dried up from the earth." The first day of the month is wane [1].

In Exodus 10-15, "Our livestock too must go with us; not a hoof is to be left behind. We have to use some of them in worshiping THE LORD our GOD". "The Israelites journeyed from Rameses to Succoth. There were about six hundred thousand men on foot, besides women and children. Many other people went up with them, as well as large droves of livestock, both flocks and herds" [10]. 海洋 sea, ocean and marine have 氵 water and 每 each ram 羊, because "not a hoof is to be left behind". Sea has ea of each, ocean has eac of each as well as oc of ox, and marine has ram in multilingual match. 牛 ox is related to oc/co, cut in comparable halves 半, when Abraham worshiped with a heifer in Genesis 15:10. 共 co has ox head with horns 屮 and both hands in coordination. 八 octo of October, octagon and octahedron is also a number based on division 分. To the surprise, ocean is related to economy in etymology, since economy has oceon of ocean and is thrifty rift and fire of each of offered flock and livestock.

The biggest miracle to Moses was to divide Red sea. In Exodus 14:23-15:21, "When Pharaoh's horses, chariots and horsemen went into the sea, THE LORD brought the waters of the sea back over them". "Miriam the prophetess, Aaron's sister, took a tambourine in her hand, and all the women followed her, with tambourines and dancing." Miriam sang to them: "Sing to THE LORD, for HE IS HIGHLY EXALTED. The horse and its rider HE has hurled into the sea." This anecdote has to dance. 軼 anecdote has 車 vehicle and loss 失, as "HE made the wheels of their chariots come off so that they had difficulty driving." "The water flowed back and covered the chariots and horsemen". Miriam has mari of marine and mira of miracle.

舞 龘 dance has the leading dancer Miriam 大, 廿廿 two ox heads and ✲✲ firewood to represent burnt offering, and two steps 舛 to represent dancing feet or women following Miriam. Because of burnt offering, dance is related to candle in etymology, with can as an affix of burning. In addition, dance has cean of ocean and is related to absence 無, a Latin and French-derived word in multiple languages. In definitive multilingual biblical match of etymology, 無 (橆 as its ancient version) absence is sea dance (bance), since Pharaoh's horses and horsemen were lost in Red sea. 嫵 lovely gesture of woman refers to Miriam's dancing, rather than no woman 無女. These are typical examples of words created not according to human common sense but to match bible.

無 no, null and annul have no bull, as 大 people burn ox 丷 to ashes on firewood ⽊⽊. Worshipers fondle 撫 bulls with fond 憮, as these bulls will be sacrificed on altar to be absent later on. "He is to lay his hand on its head and slaughter it before THE LORD". 蕪 ﷽ wasteland or uninhabited place has to burn bulls on firewood in the wild represented by grass land ⼗⼗ (⼧), as part of bull is burnt to annihilation outside of camp in sin offering [11]. 蕪 has grass ⼗⼗, ⼍人 man, 廿廾 two bulls with horns, and fire ⺣. 莫 ﷽ not is previously thought as sunset at grassland, but this testimony presents its etymology as a designated place ☉ to burn offering in the wild ⼗⼗ but not in camp. In Leviticus 4:10-12 [11], "But the hide of the bull and all its flesh, as well as the head and legs, the inner parts and offal—that is, all the rest of the bull—he must take outside the camp to a place ceremonially clean, where the ashes are thrown, and burn it in a wood fire on the ash heap." In Hebrews 13:11-12 [22], "The high priest carries the blood of animals into The Most Holy Place as a sin offering, but the bodies are burned outside the camp." In Leviticus 4:8-6:10, priest "shall remove the ashes of the burnt offering that the fire has consumed on the altar and place them beside the altar. Then he is to take off these clothes and put on others, and carry the ashes outside the camp to a place that is ceremonially clean". This is the etymology of litter, what is lit on altar.

有 (⿰ as its ancient version) presence is to separate, sever, serve and present offering 𝒫 by hand 𝒦. 有 𝓈, to have, has divided veal 𝒫, human as letter h, and ha of hand 𝒦. In additionally related etymology, the avian affix ave of have represents sacrificed dove and pigeon. Have can be plural as cattle offerings are cut to pieces and birds are often offered in pair. For example in Luke 2:22-24 [17], "When the time of their purification according to the Law of Moses had been completed, Joseph and Mary took Him to Jerusalem to present Him to THE LORD (as it is written in the Law of THE LORD, "Every firstborn male is to be consecrated to THE LORD"), and to offer a sacrifice in keeping with what is said in the Law of THE LORD: "a pair of doves or two young pigeons."" 随 to follow has hand above sacrificed meat 有 𝓈 and affixes of location 𝑓 and motion 辶, when Israelites followed GOD to offer hallow sacrifice in Exodus' migration [10]. 辶(辵 辵) is etymologically derived from the greatest human migration after great flood 彡 stopped 屮, and from 屮 motion across Red sea 彡 [1-7]. 屮 is the affix of foot that can represent go, stand or stop 止. In multilingual mutual match to biblical etymology as the origin of human words, follow has flow because of biblical water flow 彡, not simply to follow a river or spring to drink for natural survival.

3.1.8 Miracle of manna

Numerous miracles of Moses are the etymology of words [2-7]. For instance, 罐 jar/urn/can has container 缶, manna seeds (represented by a plant affix 艹), quail as a bird 隹, and altar at two places to indicate journey, when Israelites carried altar in Exodus. Manna "tasted like wafers made with honey". So desserts were provided in desert throughout the forty years.

Manna was a divine promise 許, whose ancient version 𧥣 has 午 午 to represent rain of manna as one of its interpretations, as in Exodus 16:2-35 "I will rain down bread from heaven for you". "When the dew settled on the camp at night, the manna also came". "Each morning everyone gathered as much as he needed, and when the sun grew hot, it melted away." 午 午 午 noon is when sun grows hot to be full of radiation 午. 午's dot represents manna or inhibition, while 午's horizontal line represents no, as manna melted and there was no more manna rained to ground at noon. 缶 缶 container has the rained manna 午 above container ∪ when manna rain stopped 一.

However, in Numbers 11:4-18 they still grumbled. "If only we had meat to eat! We were better off in Egypt!" 怨 grumble has worshiper 㔾 for meat 夕 in heart 心, and ramble is blamer. "THE ANGER OF THE LORD burned against the people, and HE struck them with a severe plague" at Kibroth

Hattaavah for their disobedience 忤. 摇 wobble has bowl 缶. 舂 舂 is to pound in mortar with pestle 杵. "The people went around gathering it, and then ground it in a handmill or crushed it in a mortar. They cooked it in a pot or made it into cakes." 陶 pottery is related to pot 缶 and can be washed 淘. 掏 to take out is to take manna out of pot. Manna could only be kept for a single day for the five weekdays. "No one is to keep any of it until morning", so that 罄 罄 empty has manna pot 缶.

In the direct etymology, 午 noon means non (no), no moon or no starlight. 午's dot and 午's horizontal line represent blockage, while 午 represents radiating light from night stars. In other words, noon's ancient versions 午 午 represent blocked light, because stars are not visible at noon, appearing to be blocked. However, in other words it is light from sun rather than from the other zillions of stars, for example, when 午 functions as a branch of earthly branch calendar.

午 noon is the seventh branch of the earthly branch calendar in ancient China and neighboring Asian nations, and represents 11:00-13:00, since darkness started to be over the land in Luke 23:44-45 and sunlight started to be blocked 午 午. "It was now about noon, and darkness came over the whole land until three in the afternoon, for the sun stopped shining"—the historical darkness because of Jesus Christ. All the twelve earthly branches of the Asian calendar system match the crucifixion day of The Son of GOD, Manna from heaven [7].

食 (as its ancient versions) to eat has ∆ Tent, container of manna, manna and urn, and worshiper. Its alternative biblical interpretation is altar with fire. It functions as an affix in numerous words and has Tent, because Tent of Meeting had the gold jar of manna in Exodus 16:4-35 and Hebrews 9:3-4 [10, 22]. 養 nurture has this manna urn, as "I will rain down bread from heaven for you" [10]. It gives rise to nurse, nursery, nourish, nutrient, nutriment and nutrition.

鶉 quail has ∧ camp, district 口 and person to enjoy 享, and is related to liquid in a journey to enjoy urn of manna, as in Exodus 16:1-32 "That evening quail came and covered the camp. In the morning the ground around the camp was covered with dew" and "thin flakes appeared". "Israel called the bread manna." 露 dew is to 霝 雨 rain manna on road 路 where Israelites dwelt. 蔽 cover has that represents hand to collect manna after manna rain. Addition of two hands will turn it to 弊, malpractice without abiding by regulation, since Moses required that "no one is to keep any of it until morning" but "some of them paid no attention to Moses; they kept part of it until morning, but it was full of maggots and began to smell". The outdated leftover 敆 had to be cast away 撇.

Manna is logical necessity. Forty years of migration for a thousand of miles by two million people requires gigantic amounts of food and water supply in desert. Even lacking food for a few days would be devastating. However, during such a critical time, they enacted such a unique decree of clean and unclean food to forbid eating most edibles, because this decree was from GOD.

Among the multiple interpretations, 享 enjoy has 亼 tent and 孚, who can be interpreted as a junior person. To enjoy has join (joen/joyn), twin babies. In etymology, junior is related to join, because Jacob joined Esau in delivery. In Genesis 25:24, "When the time came for her to give birth, there were twin boys in her womb. The first to come out was red, and his whole body was like a hairy garment; so they named him Esau. After this, his brother came out, with his hand grasping Esau's heel; so he was named Jacob." 幼 junior has 厶 in pair to indicate this touch, and an arm for Jacob's hand 力. Junior, juvenile, young, adjunct, junction, join, adjoin and joint are related words.

3.1.9 Liquid and quail in quarrel

After quail, came quarrel, which has quael of quail, as people quarreled with Moses on lack of additional taste before quail was provided. "They camped at Rephidim" and "quarreled with Moses" for water supply, so that quabble has aqu and lequab of liquid, and quarrel has aqua (water in Latin) and lequa of liquid from quarry, where rock is obtained. In Genesis 13:5-8 "quarreling arose between Abram's herdsmen and the herdsmen of Lot." So Abram said to Lot, "Let's not have any quarreling between you and me, or between your herdsmen and mine, for we are brothers."

塞 𡎚, to fill in, has tent ⌐, two hands, 土 earth and jamming items 工. In Genesis 26:15-33, "all the wells that his father's servants had dug", "Philistines stopped up, filling them with earth" [1]. Isaac "encamped in the valley of Gerar and settled there. Isaac reopened the wells that had been dug in the time of his father Abraham, which the Philistines had stopped up". At Beersheba, "Isaac built an altar", "pitched his tent, and there his servants dug a well". 池 well has 也 as well. 寨 village was often to dwell near well 井. Well is where ell (flock or herd [3]) drinks water. Letter w represents water. In Genesis 29:2 Jacob "saw a well in the field, with three flocks of sheep lying near it because the flocks were watered from that well" [1]. People often greeted each other "Are you well?" near the well, like Laban greeted Jacob. This is the biblical basis for such greeting in cultural anthropology and archaeology.

3.1.10 Bronze snake

乞 beg has 人 human being and snake 乚, as people begged GOD to take the snakes away in Numbers 21:6-9, when "snakes bit them. Many of the people died" [12]. "So Moses prayed for the people. ""Make a snake. Put it up on a pole. Then anyone who is bitten can look at it and remain alive". So Moses made a bronze snake and put it up on a pole. Then when anyone was bitten by a snake and looked at the bronze snake, he lived." 吊 condole resembles snake on pole. 活 survival has 舌 已 considered by linguists as snake's tongue to bite people, although its alternative interpretation is served offering on altar. To survive is to serve. 在 扗 presence has the pole of serpent 才 next to ground 土, as people could be alive by looking at it. It is related to presence 存, which has the nailed Son 子, as in 1 John 2:15-3:14 "Just as Moses lifted up the snake in the wilderness, so the Son of Man must be lifted up" [18]. Son's most frequent type of miracle is healing, which links to the bronze snake lifted by Moses as symbol of medicine.

3.2. Priest

3.2.1 Etymology of priest

祭 worship has offered meat 夕, priest's hand 又, and a known affix of divine altar 示 with division of offering ハ. 祭司 (鼎 冏) priest has sacrificed offering 夕, hand 又 and 示 altar with division of offering ハ. Priest is to sever and serve burnt offering in pair and pieces, as described in Genesis and Leviticus [1, 11]. This is priest's prestige. Preach is char par, burn the pair by priest. Worship has multiple interpretations. Worship is worth split, worth splitting burnt offering. Worship is water (w) person (or) ship, as the first thing that Noah performed was worship by burnt offering on altar after coming out of ark [1].

Praise GOD! Priests raise hands to praise GOD. Praise is a typical word for the cut in pair, the theological method of Abraham in worship. Praise has pair to separate, and divine is to divide offering. 赞 praise currently has two priests 𝑅 𝑅 and bulls 牛 , and its ancient version had divided hoof represented by symmetry in footstep, as clean land offering "has a split hoof

48

completely divided and that chews the cud" [11, 13]. This regulation also restricts diet to clean food [11, 13], so that food is double hoof with foot of fission, and beef is divided hoof as burnt offering. Offer has divided foot in addition to two hands as etymology, and feast in festival has feasible diet of fission in piety. 赞 praise also has the separated pair of offering 贝 (Written versions: simplified 贝, traditional 貝, ancient � 貝), which represents the affix of wealth in words such as price 價 and purchase 购/購. Sharing the same affix in pair, 贊 praise, 價 price, and 購 purchase have definitive bilingual mutual match in the languages. Such precise "coincidence" in mutual and biblical etymological match can only be achieved by CREATOR. In this way, we prove THE CREATOR.

祘 GOD shines from cloud 云. In Exodus 40:34-38 "the cloud covered the Tent of Meeting, and THE GLORY OF THE LORD filled the tabernacle" [10]. In the prayer to GOD in Numbers 6:22-27 [12], "THE LORD bless you and keep you; THE LORD make HIS FACE shine upon you and be gracious to you; THE LORD turn HIS FACE toward you and give you peace." Thus, in etymology pray has ray, and the additional etymology of the divine affix 示 礻 is radiant light from divine cloud.

Spirit can be regrouped as priist of priest, because priest is spiritual. Spirit has iris as a potential affix of rainbow. 靈 spirit has rainbow 雨工 (虹 rainbow's affix) and two worshipers 人人 from place to place as represented by altar at three places 口口口, because in Genesis 7:4-9:17 "Whenever the rainbow appears in the clouds, I will see it and remember the everlasting covenant between GOD and all living creatures of every kind on the earth" [1]. The simplified version of spirit 灵 has hand ⺕ above fire 火, consistent with biblical burnt offering too.

3.2.2 Administration

President has priest and is the priest of residents. President is high priest. Priest praises GOD in piety. Prime minister is priest of ministry in administration, secretary is to section sacred offering, and office is to offer sacrifice. Department is to cut meat to parts as bureau of burnt offering. 党 party is to cut in pair 丿乀 and to parts for altar 口, and must serve GOD. As partners, priests participate, partake and take part in worship.

Politic is to split. In addition, politic is to burn lipo, lipid, like Abel, Moses and Aaron worshiped [1, 10]. In Leviticus 4:10-35, "He shall burn all the fat on the altar". In Genesis 4:4 "Abel brought fat portions from some of the firstborn of his flock. THE LORD looked with favor on Abel and his offering". When favoring a biblical man because of his righteous faith and action, GOD would favor his offering. Thus, GOD does not show favorism of bias [19, 23]. In etymology, bias is side, to choose a side, a word in human application. According to the sent Jesus Christ, mercy is more important than sacrifice. In multilingual biblical match, 政 politic is related to positive 正. 正 ⻊ 𞠶 positive, poise situ, is 止 pause in situ, because of prohibition (一) of stepping (止) onto the holiest place. In alternative interpretation, 正 positive is to position a worshiper in front of altar. Politic and policy are related to polis of metropolis, and city 市 巿, polis in Greek, also has 亠 offering on altar 冂. 公 citizens cut and slice offering together, as indicated by division 八 and fire 厶. To indicate is to dice, cide and divide dedicated cattle. In multilingual biblical match, 政 politic and police 警 share the affix of hand in offering 攵 攴. Politely and courteously in the biblical courtyard, 警察 police is to slice offering and burn lipid in front of Tent of Meeting 冂 for 敬 respectful worship 祭, and guard the worshiping place within camp, Tent of Meeting next to burnt altar [11, 12]. Such words are in obvious biblical etymology, definitely proving divine creation.

官 bureaucrat (𠂤 𠂤 𠂤 as its ancient version) can go from one area to another area (as represented by $\mathcal{E}$) of the holy building Tabernacle ∩, where other people are forbidden to enter. In other words, in etymology bureaucrat is related to tabernacle as biblical priest. As bureau is also in French and Latin-derived languages, this is a multilingual biblical match.

蝙蝠 bat has tab of tabernacle 戶, as its wings were created to resemble a set of curtains 幅, and when it stands its wings resemble tabernacle, Tent of Meeting. This creature is fully reflected by biblical etymology, similar to the words of other creatures that reflect biblical etymology [2-7].

3.2.3 Profession

雇 to employ has emplo of temple 戶/殿 [5], 職 career has ear 耳 for consecration, and 聘 hire is part of shrine with consecrated right ear 耳 [10, 11]. Swear has ear and wear, blood on earlobe and sacred garments to wear, when biblical priests are sworn into office in inauguration in Exodus [10]. "Fasten the ephod on him by its skillfully woven waistband", and "take some of its blood and put it on the lobes of the right ears of Aaron and his sons". Worker is worshiper. Labor is to burn lamb. Industry is to construct Tent of Meeting from tricolor yarn [10]. 農 peasant is to step away from saint land of Eden [1]. 商 business (�? ? as its ancient versions) is to combust incense, sin and burnt offerings near altar 口 to worship GOD 帝 ? ?. 商 also represents the ancient Shang dynasty of China, around the historical time of Exodus when LORD frequently arrived in cloud ? [1, 10-12]. With ax 斧, 兵 soldiers of Israelites dissected flock and herd as division of GOD [10, 11].

Profession is pro confession, as in Leviticus 5:5-6 "When anyone is guilty in any of these ways, he must confess in what way he has sinned" "and the priest shall make atonement for him" [11]. Professor is pro confessor as a priest, laboratory has labor at altar, and experiment is to cut offered meat in pair. Scho of schizophrenia means split. Modern medical diagnosis of "schizophrenia" includes hearing unusual voice, seeing unusual vision, and having running and intruding thought, but these were all exactly what many biblical people and prophets experienced based on holy bible. The symptoms of mental patients healed by Jesus were triggered by Legion and additional spirits that attached [15-18], rather than from their own physiology. Throughout the entire old testament, only a king was recorded to have significant but intermittent mental disorder attacked by Satan, but in three years so many mental patients were attacked by spirits, like the attack to Job to test his faith, in order for Jesus to heal to glorify His FATHER

THE GOD. Thus, true mental illness is extremely rare, and the definition and treatment in psychiatry and psychology should be reformed, although Jesus mentioned no miracle necessary except the sign of Jonah, so that there is little chance to misdiagnose and treat a biblical prophet with schizophrenia with profit-driven drugs, when direct prophet does not even exist anymore because "all the prophets and the law prophesied until John" [15]. Scholar splits ox near altar and burns cholesterol, as "He shall burn all the fat on the altar" [11]. Seminar has to cut to halves like Abraham did [1], as semi means halves.

With Tent of Meeting in side view ⌐ ⌐, priests are faculty to cut calf, and factory 廠 is faction and fraction in front of divine facility to cut offering to pieces for burnt altar. Technology and technique are to cut and roast meat at theological kitchen. Thesis is theological. Theory is theological. Teacher is to char at altar and eat inherited portion of charred offering [11, 12].

As an apparent bilingual match, 薪 salary links to celery 芹, as celery was created to resemble firewood cut by axe 斧, and priest's salary is burnt offering on firewood. "This is the portion of the offerings made to THE LORD by fire that were allotted to Aaron and his sons" and "Israelites give this to them as their regular share" [11, 12]. Wage is for priests to wave offering as their share.

Ax/axe 斤 斤's 斤 is similar to ㄅ of an affix of weapon (ㄉ 刂), which also means weight of about one pound. Its overall structure can be considered as detachment of leather from ox, an early step in burnt offering [11]. 斬 execution has axe to cut, although it is to execute burnt offering. 例 example has axe as a weapon 刂, which is also in exam 測. To examine is to split offering with axe, as priests should examine the cut offering and separate fat from the rest to offer only the required parts [11]. 新 new has this weapon 斤, and weapon has new. 祈 祈 pray has to cut offering in pair and doublet 八 with ax/hatchet 斤. This method of biblical burnt offering, like Abraham did in Genesis 15:10, answers the other etymology of pray to have pair.

In etymology, income is related to economic and economy, which have y/income. Menu, income and economy are related to offering [6]. Value is veal. Capital is cattle at altar. To revere GOD and sever offering is revenue. Expense is incense. Price is spice. Tax has ax and altar. 八 divided offering is in tax 稅, which has 禾 grain offering and division at altar by worshiper 儿. 利 profit has similar etymology, although ax is substituted with the affix of weapon 刂. Pro fission is profit. To divide offering is dividend.

IV. Discussion

This testimony presents the biblical etymology of prophet and priest, as well as numerous words with the miracles of the greatest prophet and priest Moses as their semantic origin. For instance, word linkage analysis indicates that many words are interconnected in logic chain to match the miracle of manna, indicating that the daily provision of manna was a true historical event [2-7]. Anthropologists and archaeologists always want to find evidence for the miracles recorded by Moses in Exodus, but such evidence is already extensively embedded in the analyzed or to-be-analyzed words of human languages [2-7].

New affix of scepter is presented to match Moses' staff of snake 蛇, solving thousands of years of semantic puzzles for a number of words such as affiliation 属 and wind 風. "Moses stretched out his hand over the sea, and all that night THE LORD drove the sea back with a strong east wind and turned it into dry land" [10]. Words often have more than one biblical etymologies. For example, wind's main etymology is for water to dwindle to have no water. "HE sent a wind over the earth, and the water receded" [1]. The semantic evidence is so abundant and apparent that the etymology of the majority of words in dictionaries must be revised according to bible. The discovery that ancient words share bible as their common etymology is a revolutionary conclusion.

The affix of disease 疒 has one side of offered ox, goat or sheep ㇉, which was interpreted in the past as bed instead, because human languages were divinely confused in large scale in Genesis 11, which is reflected by numerous words [2-7]. One etymology of epidemic and pandemic is to kill (-cide) bird for its blood (m) in offering. The etymology of infection is to confine, inflammation is in flame, plague is to leave to go to another place, hospital is distal site, pharmacy is away from camp, drug is to go, and quarantine is four plus ten. 醫 medicine has a water container 酉 to hold blood of the killed (-cide 殳) bird, and the outside (區 region's affix 匚) represented by arrow 矢, because leprosy patients are quarantined outside of camp [11]. Therapy is to heat offering and tear apart garment, to treat is to heat, 療 heal is to heat 燎, and disease is to segregate aside. Sick is to scki (schi, divide) burnt offering, whose root is also in schizophrenia, scissor and sickle. 病 disease is to go out of a gathering place (一) to be diverged (人) to outside region 冂. Thus, the entire range of medical terms in dictionaries matches Leviticus in etymology, unambiguously proving creation.

祈 祇 pray has par and axe 斤, as offering was cut in pair and to parts and their blood was sprayed [1]. In etymology, pray also has people in ray, not only because the leading prayer Moses' face was radiant in Exodus 34:29-30 [10], but also mainly because of the prayer to GOD in Numbers 6:22-27 after worshipers cut and burnt offering [12]. "This is how you are to bless the Israelites": "THE LORD bless you and keep you; THE LORD make HIS FACE shine upon you and be gracious to you; THE LORD turn HIS FACE toward you and give you peace."

In etymology, miracle is related to marine because of crossing Red sea, and wonder is no water when crossing this sea on dry ground. Woman's lovely gesture 嫵 refers to Miriam's dancing, solving thousands of years of linguistic puzzle on why this word has no woman 無女. These are typical examples of words created not according to human common sense but to match bible. Bible solves numerous word riddles.

The extensive multilingual match to the call to Moses indicates that it was a real historical event, and words had been divinely created ahead of time to match this biblical event [2-7]. Although GOD only started to call Abraham and Moses when they were seventy-five to eighty years old, words still extensively match these two prophets [2-7]. Words were already created before Moses wrote the initial bible, definitively indicating divine creation and specific predestination, as an essential conclusion in not only linguistic anthropology but also philosophy.

職 career has ear, and to swear also has ear 耳 [4, 5], as priests are inaugurated in consecration ceremony after blood on earlobes [4, 5]. Swear also has to wear, as biblical priests were sworn into office with sacred garments in Exodus. 聘 employment has temple, and hire is in shrine for identical reason. 雇 hire has cherubim 隹 under tabernacle 戶 to further indicate the definitive biblical etymology for words related to career and employment. For thousands of years, linguists were puzzled by why bird under a building was to hire. Such word riddles are solved in the twenty-first century by definitive multilingual biblical etymology. Thus, the testimony has verified the divine origin of languages claimed in Genesis, and validated the revealed Pentateuch and gospel books. In this way, the testimony proves THE CREATOR.

This testimony presents linguistic evidence that the etymology of prophet and priest is biblical, and answers an array of linguistic mysteries regarding etymology of words. Multilingual mutual match in etymology from holy bible is a revolutionary conclusion in linguistic anthropology and archaeology, and will have great impact on civilization and culture. The definitive evidence of word creation for biblical truth further encourages us to fully love GOD and accordingly, to love each other as brothers and sisters as one integrated United Nations. The bilingual and multilingual match in biblical etymology definitively proves divine creation as the origin of language, validates historical biblical records, and thus proves THE CREATOR.

Acknowledgement

61

We are grateful to GOD THE LORD CREATOR with full gratitude in the highest respect.

References

1. Moses. (2nd millennium B.C.). Genesis.

2. Du, J. X. (2019). Bilingual dissection of words with biblical correlation. International Journal of Language and Linguistics, 7(1): 50-4. https://doi.org/10.11648/j.ijll.20190701.17.

3. Du, J. X. (2019). Bilingual match to biblical flood. International Journal of Linguistics, 11(1): 196-216. https://doi.org/10.5296/ijl.v11i1.14434.

4. Du, J. X. (2019). Seven days, numbers and heavenly Stems. International Journal of Linguistics, 11(2): 107-51. https://doi.org/10.5296/ijl.v11i2.14755.

5. Du, J. X. (2020). Biblical etymology of tabernacle and altar. International Journal of Linguistics, 12(3): 9-27. https://doi.org/10.5296/ijl.v12i3.17012

6. Du, J. X. (2020). Biblical etymology of organs and body parts. English Literature and Language Review, 6(5): 69-90. https://doi.org/10.32861/ellr.65.69.91

7. Du, J. X. (2020). Biblical etymology of earthly branches and Jesus Christ. SocArXiv. https://doi.org/10.31235/osf.io/r9mdz

8. Du, J. X. (2020). Jesus Is Son of GOD. LawArXiv.

https://doi.org/10.31228/osf.io/48nyx

9. Du, J. X. (2020). Jesus Christ demands good deeds — Faith and action is

required for eternal life. SocArXiv. https://doi.org/10.31235/osf.io/ba4cg

10. Moses. (2nd millennium B.C.). Exodus.

11. Moses. (2nd millennium B.C.). Leviticus.

12. Moses. (2nd millennium B.C.). Numbers.

13. Moses. (2nd millennium B.C.). Deuteronomy.

14. Unknown author. (1st millennium B.C.). 2 Kings.

15. Matthew. (1st century). Matthew.

16. Mark. (1st century). Mark.

17. Luke. (1st century). Luke.

18. John. (1st century). John.

19. Unknown author. (1st century). Acts.

20. Xu, Shen. (100-121 A.D.). Analytical Dictionary of Characters.

21. Joshua. (2nd millennium B.C.). Joshua.

22. Paul. (1st century). Hebrews.

23. Paul. (1st century). Romans.

www.ingramcontent.com/pod-product-compliance
Lightning Source LLC
Chambersburg PA
CBHW050616160726
48003CB00003B/1209